D1391952

MARKS &
SPENCER

puddings
& desserts

simple and delicious easy-to-make recipes

Lorraine Turner

Marks and Spencer p.l.c.
Baker Street, London, W1U 8EP

www.marksandspencer.com

Titles in this series are subject to availability

ISBN: 1-84273-845-3

Printed in China

Produced by the Bridgewater Book Company Ltd.

Photographer Calvey Taylor-Haw

Home Economist Ruth Pollock

The crockery featured on the following pages can be
purchased at Marks and Spencer's stores:

page 19 – white bowl with silver trim, 02148/5306

page 55 – 'Yellow Rose' plate

page 57 – white bowl, 02733/4286

page 81 – 'Wild Fruits' bowl, 02148/8157109

NOTES FOR THE READER

- This book uses both metric and imperial measurements. Follow the same units of measurement throughout; do not mix metric and imperial.

- All spoon measurements are level: teaspoons are assumed to be 5 ml, and tablespoons are assumed to be 15 ml.

- Unless otherwise stated, milk is assumed to be full fat, eggs and individual vegetables such as potatoes are medium, and pepper is freshly ground black pepper.

- Recipes using raw or very lightly cooked eggs should be avoided by infants, the elderly, pregnant women, convalescents, and anyone suffering from an illness.

- The times given are an approximate guide only. Preparation times differ according to the techniques used by different people and the cooking times may also vary from those given. Optional ingredients, variations or serving suggestions have not been included in the calculations.

contents

introduction

There is nothing quite like a pudding or dessert to round off a meal. A successful dessert is always irresistible, and the ever-widening range of delicious ingredients available nowadays has brought newer and even more exciting flavours to our tables.

This book is bursting with delicious recipes. You will recognise some traditional favourites, such as Sticky Toffee Pudding, Banoffee Pie, Bakewell Tart and Apricot Crumble. There is also a tempting selection of contemporary and international dishes for you to try, such as Rose Petal Ice Cream or Toffee Bananas. Chocolate-lovers will be unable to resist the Chocolate Cherry Gateau and the Rich Chocolate Mousses, and the health-conscious among you will enjoy some of the fruit desserts or lighter concoctions such as Summer Pudding, Baked Peaches with Orange Liqueur Cream, and the Peach & Banana Sorbet.

All the recipes in this book are accompanied by lavish full-colour photographs and clear, step-by-step instructions to ensure perfect desserts every time. So whether you are catering for a large dinner party, a few family members or just for yourself, there will be something in this book to suit every occasion and every taste.

guide to recipe key	
very easy	Recipes are graded as follows: 1 pea = easy; 2 peas = very easy; 3 peas = extremely easy.
serves 4	Recipes generally serve four people. Simply halve the ingredients to serve two, taking care not to mix metric and imperial measurements.
10 minutes	Preparation time. Where marinating or soaking are involved, these times have been added on separately: eg, 15 minutes + 30 minutes to marinate.
10 minutes	Cooking time. Cooking times do not include the cooking of side dishes or accompaniments served with the main dishes.

golden pudding
page 12

peach and strawberry tart
page 42

stuffed pears
page 54

cherry baskets
page 80

puddings
& cakes

Where would we be without comforting
puddings and tempting cakes? The recipes
in this chapter are a feast for the senses and
the taste buds. From Individual Chocolate
Puddings and Creamy Rice Pudding to
Apple Upside-down Cake and Jam Roly Poly,
these dishes are easy to prepare and a
delight to cook. They are full of irresistible
ingredients and flavours, and provide a
satisfying treat in themselves or a
wonderful finish to any meal.

sticky toffee pudding

very easy	
serves 4	
10–15 minutes	
35–40 minutes	

ingredients

PUDDING
75 g/2¾ oz sultanas
150 g/5½ oz stoned dates, chopped
1 tsp bicarbonate of soda
2 tbsp butter, plus extra for greasing
200 g/7 oz brown sugar
2 eggs
200 g/7 oz self-raising flour, sifted

STICKY TOFFEE SAUCE
2 tbsp butter
175 ml/6 fl oz double cream
200 g/7 oz brown sugar

zested orange rind, to decorate

freshly whipped cream, to serve

To make the pudding, put the fruits and bicarbonate of soda into a heatproof bowl. Cover with boiling water and leave to soak.

Preheat the oven to 180°C/350°F/Gas Mark 4. Grease a round cake tin, 20 cm/8 inches in diameter, with butter. Put the remaining butter in a separate bowl, add the sugar and mix well. Beat in the eggs then fold in the flour. Drain the soaked fruits, add to the bowl and mix. Spoon the mixture evenly into the prepared cake tin. Transfer to the preheated oven and bake for 35–40 minutes. The pudding is cooked when a skewer inserted into the centre comes out clean. About 5 minutes before the end of the cooking time, make the sauce. Melt the butter in a saucepan over a medium heat. Stir in the cream and sugar and bring to the boil, stirring constantly. Lower the heat and simmer for 5 minutes.

Turn out the pudding onto a serving plate and pour over the sauce. Decorate with zested orange rind and serve with whipped cream.

individual chocolate puddings

easy	
serves 4	
10–15 minutes	
50 minutes	

ingredients

PUDDINGS	CHOCOLATE SAUCE
100 g/3½ oz caster sugar	2 tbsp unsalted butter
3 eggs	100 g/3½ oz plain chocolate
75 g/2¾ oz plain flour, sifted	5 tbsp water
50 g/1¾ oz cocoa powder, sifted	1 tbsp caster sugar
100 g/3½ oz unsalted butter, melted, plus extra for greasing	1 tbsp coffee-flavoured liqueur, such as Kahlua
100 g/3½ oz plain chocolate, melted	coffee beans, to decorate

To make the puddings, put the sugar and eggs into a heatproof bowl and place over a saucepan of simmering water. Whisk for about 10 minutes until frothy. Remove the bowl from the heat and fold in the flour and cocoa powder. Fold in the butter, then the chocolate. Mix well. Grease 4 small pudding basins with butter. Spoon the mixture into the basins and cover with greaseproof paper. Top with foil and secure with string. Place the puddings in a large saucepan filled with enough simmering water to reach halfway up the sides of the basins. Steam for about 40 minutes or until cooked through.

About 2–3 minutes before the end of the cooking time, make the sauce. Put the butter, chocolate, water and sugar into a small saucepan and warm over a low heat, stirring constantly, until melted together. Stir in the liqueur.

Remove the puddings from the heat, turn out into serving dishes and pour over the sauce. Decorate with coffee beans and serve.

golden pudding

very easy	
serves 4–6	
10–15 minutes	
1½ hours	

ingredients

3 tbsp butter, plus extra for greasing
2 tbsp caster sugar
2 eggs
6 tbsp plain flour, sifted
1 tsp baking powder, sifted
6 tbsp milk

1 tsp vanilla essence
4 tbsp golden syrup

thin strips of crystallised orange peel,
   to decorate

hot custard, to serve

Lightly grease a 850-ml/1½-pint pudding basin with butter. Put the remaining butter into a bowl with the sugar, and cream together until fluffy. Add the eggs and beat together well. Mix in the flour and baking powder, then stir in the milk and vanilla essence. Continue to stir until smooth.

Pour the golden syrup into the pudding basin, then spoon the pudding mixture on top. Cover with greaseproof paper and top with a piece of aluminium foil, tied on securely with string. Transfer to a large saucepan filled with enough simmering water to reach halfway up the sides of the pudding basin. Simmer gently for about 1½ hours until cooked right through, topping up the water level when necessary.

Lift out the pudding and leave to rest for 5 minutes, then turn it out onto a serving plate. Decorate with thin strips of crystallised orange peel and serve hot with custard.

jam roly poly

easy	
serves 4	
20 minutes	
1 ½ hours	

ingredients

175 g/6 oz self-raising flour, plus extra
  for dusting
pinch of salt
75 g/2¾ oz shredded suet
3–4 tbsp hot water
6 tbsp raspberry jam

2 tbsp milk
1 tbsp butter, for greasing

raspberries, to decorate

custard, to serve

Put the flour and salt into a bowl and mix together well. Add the suet, then stir in enough hot water to make a light dough. Using your hands, shape the dough into a ball. Turn out the dough onto a lightly floured work surface and knead gently until smooth. Roll out into a rectangle about 28 cm/11 inches x 23 cm/9 inches.

Spread the jam over the dough, leaving a border of about 1 cm/ ½ inch all round. Brush the border with milk. Starting with the short side, roll up the dough evenly until you have one large roll.

Lightly grease a large piece of aluminium foil with butter, then place the dough roll in the centre. Gently close up the foil around the dough, allowing room for expansion, and seal tightly. Transfer to a steamer on top of a pan of boiling water. Steam for about 1 ½ hours until cooked, topping up the water level when necessary.

Turn out the roly poly onto a serving platter and decorate with raspberries. Serve with hot custard.

creamy rice pudding

very easy

serves 4

10–15 minutes

2 ½ hours

ingredients

1 tbsp butter, for greasing
85 g/3 oz sultanas
5 tbsp caster sugar
90 g/3 ¼ oz pudding rice
1.2 litres/2 pints milk

1 tsp vanilla essence
finely grated rind of 1 large lemon
pinch of freshly grated nutmeg

chopped pistachio nuts, to decorate

Preheat the oven to 160°C/325°F/Gas Mark 3. Grease an 850-ml/ 1 ½-pint ovenproof dish with butter.

Put the sultanas, sugar and rice into a mixing bowl, then stir in the milk and vanilla essence. Transfer to the prepared dish, sprinkle over the grated lemon rind and the nutmeg, then bake in the preheated oven for 2 ½ hours.

Remove from the oven and transfer to individual serving bowls. Decorate with chopped pistachio nuts and serve.

eve's pudding

very easy	
serves 4	
15 minutes	
45 minutes	

ingredients

100 g/3½ oz butter
500 g/1 lb 2 oz cooking apples, peeled
  and cored
1 tbsp lemon juice
150 g/5½ oz caster sugar
1 tsp ground mixed spice
40 g/1½ oz sultanas

25 g/1 oz currants
1 egg, beaten
150 g/5½ oz self-raising flour, sifted
2–3 tbsp milk

chopped mixed nuts, to decorate

double cream, to serve

Preheat the oven to 180°C/350°F/Gas Mark 4. Grease an 850-ml/ 1½-pint ovenproof dish with a little butter.

Slice the cooking apples and put them into a bowl with the lemon juice. Stir the apples gently to coat them in the lemon juice. Sprinkle over half of the sugar, then add the mixed spice, sultanas and currants. Mix together well, then spoon the mixture into the prepared ovenproof dish.

In a separate bowl, cream together the remaining butter and sugar, then gradually mix in the beaten egg. Fold in the flour, then stir in enough milk to give the mixture a light, dropping consistency. Transfer to the ovenproof dish and spread evenly over the fruit. Scatter over the chopped nuts and bake in the preheated oven for 45 minutes until golden.

Remove from the oven and serve hot with double cream.

summer pudding

easy

serves 4–6

20 minutes
+ 2–8 hours
to chill

5 minutes

ingredients

200 g/7 oz strawberries, hulled
  and quartered
200 g/7 oz blueberries
200 g/7 oz raspberries
200 g/7 oz cranberries
200 g/7 oz blackberries
6 tbsp caster sugar
2 tbsp lemon juice
2 tbsp sherry

1 tsp ground mixed spice
8 medium slices of day-old white
  bread, crusts removed

whole strawberries, blueberries,
  raspberries, cranberries and
  blackberries, to decorate

double cream, to serve (optional)

Put the fruit into a saucepan over a medium heat. Stir in the sugar, lemon juice, sherry and mixed spice. Heat for 5 minutes until the sugar has dissolved. Remove from the heat and leave to cool.

Cut the bread diagonally into quarters, then use it to line the bottom and sides of an 850-ml/1½-pint pudding basin, keeping a few pieces to one side (you may need to trim some of the pieces to fit). Spoon the cooled berry mixture into the prepared pudding basin and cover with the remaining bread. Place the basin inside a shallow bowl to catch any overflowing juices, then top with a small plate that fits snugly inside the rim of the basin. Place a large can of food on top to weigh the plate down, then refrigerate for at least 2 hours, but preferably overnight.

To serve, remove the can and plate, loosen the sides of the pudding with a knife, then turn out onto a serving plate. Decorate with berries and serve with double cream, if using.

bread & butter pudding

		ingredients
very easy		

very easy

serves 4

15 minutes

40 minutes

ingredients

6 medium slices of day-old wholemeal
   bread, crusts removed
2 tbsp butter
2 tbsp sugar
25 g/1 oz sultanas

25 g/1 oz currants
425 ml/15 fl oz milk
2 eggs
½ tsp ground mixed spice

Preheat the oven to 180°C/350°F/Gas Mark 4. Spread the slices of bread with butter, then cut each slice into quarters. Arrange half of the bread, buttered side up, on the bottom of an 850-ml/1½-pint ovenproof dish. Sprinkle over half of the sugar, then scatter over half of the sultanas and currants. Top with the remaining bread, then sprinkle over the remaining sugar and fruit.

Pour the milk into a large mixing bowl. Add the eggs and mixed spice and whisk until smooth. Pour the mixture evenly over the bread, then transfer to the preheated oven and bake for about 40 minutes. Remove from the oven and serve hot.

apple upside-down cake

ingredients

700 g/1 lb 9 oz cooking apples
8 cloves
140 g/5 oz butter
250 g/9 oz caster sugar
2 eggs
25 g/1 oz flaked almonds,
  lightly toasted

25 g/1 oz hazelnuts, lightly toasted
  and ground
125 ml/4 fl oz double cream
125 ml/4 fl oz milk
½ tsp ground mixed spice
150 g/5½ oz self-raising flour, sifted

double cream, to serve

Preheat the oven to 180°C/350°F/Gas Mark 4. Bring a large
saucepan of water to the boil. Peel and core the apples, cut into
slices, then add them to the pan with the cloves. Lower the heat
and simmer for 5 minutes, then remove from the heat. Drain well.
Discard the cloves. Leave the apple to cool a little.

Grease a 20-cm/8-inch diameter cake tin with butter. Arrange the
cooked apple slices over the bottom of the tin and sprinkle over
2 tablespoons of the sugar. In a separate bowl, cream together the
remaining butter and sugar. Gradually mix in the eggs, then the
nuts, cream, milk and mixed spice. Gradually beat in the flour until
smooth. Spread the mixture evenly over the apples, then bake the
cake in the preheated oven for about 40 minutes, until golden.
The cake is cooked when a skewer inserted into the centre comes
out clean. Remove from the oven and leave to cool for 5 minutes,
then turn out onto a serving plate. Serve hot with double cream.

chocolate cherry gateau

easy

makes one
23-cm/9-inch
cake

15 minutes
+ 30 minutes
to cool

50–55
minutes

ingredients

3 tbsp unsalted butter, melted, plus
  extra for greasing
900 g/2 lb fresh cherries, stoned
  and halved
250 g/9 oz caster sugar
100 ml/3½ fl oz cherry brandy
100 g/3½ oz plain flour
50g/1¾ oz cocoa powder

½ tsp baking powder
4 eggs
1 litre/1¾ pints double cream

DECORATION
grated dark chocolate
whole fresh cherries

Preheat the oven to 180°C/350°F/Gas Mark 4. Grease and line
a 23-cm/9-inch springform cake tin. Put the cherries into a
saucepan, add 3 tablespoons of the sugar and the cherry brandy.
Simmer for 5 minutes. Drain, reserving the syrup. In another bowl,
sift together the flour, cocoa and baking powder.

Put the eggs in a heatproof bowl and beat in 160 g/5¾ oz of the
sugar. Place the bowl over a pan of simmering water and beat for
6 minutes or until thickened. Remove from the heat, then
gradually fold in the flour mixture and melted butter. Spoon into
the cake tin. Bake for 40 minutes. Remove from the oven and leave
to cool. Turn out the cake and cut in half horizontally. Mix the
cream with the remaining sugar. Spread the reserved syrup over
the cut sides of the cake. Arrange the cherries over one half, top
with a layer of cream, and place the other half on top. Cover the
whole cake with cream, press grated chocolate all over and
decorate with cherries.

pies
& tarts

What can be more enticing than a flood of sweet fruits cascading from a warm pie, or a succulent tart studded with fruits and laced with spices? The stunning display of pies and tarts in this chapter will have every member of the household asking for more, and every dinner guest longing to be offered another piece. From the Forest Fruit Pie to the Chocolate Orange Tart, the only problem you will have with these recipes is that as soon as the serving plate is empty, your diners will want more.

forest fruit pie

easy

serves 4

20 minutes
+ 30 minutes
to rest

45 minutes

ingredients

250 g/9 oz blueberries
250 g/9 oz raspberries
250 g/9 oz blackberries
100 g/3½ oz caster sugar
200 g/7 oz plain flour, plus extra
  for dusting
25 g/1 oz ground hazelnuts
100 g/3½ oz butter, diced, plus extra
  for greasing

finely grated rind of 1 lemon
1 egg yolk, beaten
4 tbsp milk

2 tsp icing sugar, to dust

whipped cream, to serve

Put the fruit into a saucepan with 3 tablespoons of caster sugar and simmer, stirring, for 5 minutes. Remove from the heat. Sift the flour into a bowl, then add the hazelnuts. Rub in the butter, then sift in the remaining sugar. Add the lemon rind, egg yolk and 3 tablespoons of milk and mix. Turn out onto a lightly floured work surface and knead briefly. Leave to rest for 30 minutes.

Preheat the oven to 190°C/375°F/Gas Mark 5. Grease a 20-cm/ 8-inch ovenproof pie dish with butter. Roll out half the pastry to a thickness of 5 mm/¼ inch and use it to line the dish. Spoon the fruit into the pastry shell. Brush the rim with water, then roll out the remaining dough and use it to cover the pie. Trim and crimp round the edges, make 2 small slits in the top and decorate with 2 leaf shapes cut from the dough trimmings. Brush all over with the remaining milk. Bake for 40 minutes. Remove from the oven, sprinkle over the icing sugar and serve with whipped cream.

banoffee pie

	ingredients	
easy	two 400 ml/14 fl oz cans sweetened condensed milk	4 ripe bananas
	6 tbsp butter, melted	1 tbsp lemon juice
serves 4	150 g/5½ oz digestive biscuits, crushed into crumbs	1 tsp vanilla essence
	50 g/1¾ oz almonds, toasted and ground	75 g/2¾ oz chocolate, grated
20 minutes + 1 hour to cool	50 g/1¾ oz hazelnuts, toasted and ground	450 ml/16 fl oz thick double cream, whipped
2¼ hours		

Place the cans of milk in a large saucepan and cover them with water. Bring to the boil, then reduce the heat and simmer for 2 hours. Ensure the water is topped up regularly to keep the cans covered. Carefully lift out the hot cans and leave to cool.

Preheat the oven to 180°C/350°F/Gas Mark 4. Grease a 23-cm/ 9-inch flan tin with butter. Put the remaining butter into a bowl and add the biscuits and nuts. Mix together well, then press the mixture evenly into the base and sides of the flan tin. Bake for 10–12 minutes, then remove from the oven and leave to cool.

Peel and slice the bananas and put them into a bowl. Sprinkle over the lemon juice and vanilla essence and mix gently. Spread the banana mixture over the biscuit crust in the tin, then open the cans of condensed milk and spoon the contents over the bananas. Sprinkle over 50 g/1¾ oz of the chocolate, then top with a thick layer of whipped cream. Scatter over the remaining chocolate and serve.

lemon meringue pie

		ingredients	
easy		PASTRY	FILLING
		200 g/7 oz plain flour, plus extra	3 tbsp cornflour
serves 4		for dusting	300 ml/10 fl oz cold water
		100 g/3½ oz butter, diced, plus	juice and grated rind of 2 lemons
		extra for greasing	175 g/6 oz caster sugar
20 minutes		50 g/1¾ oz icing sugar, sifted	2 eggs, separated
+ 30 minutes		finely grated rind of 1 lemon	
to rest		1 egg yolk, beaten	
		3 tbsp milk	
1 hour			

To make the pastry, sift the flour into a bowl and rub in the butter. Mix in the remaining ingredients. Knead briefly on a lightly floured work surface. Leave to rest for 30 minutes. Preheat the oven to 180°C/350°F/Gas Mark 4. Grease a 20-cm/8-inch ovenproof pie dish with butter. Roll out the pastry to a thickness of 5 mm/¼ inch and use it to line the dish. Prick with a fork, line with baking paper and fill with baking beans. Bake for 15 minutes. Remove from the oven. Lower the temperature to 150°C/300°F/Gas Mark 2.

To make the filling, mix the cornflour with a little water. Put the remaining water into a pan. Stir in the lemon juice and rind and cornflour paste. Bring to the boil, stirring. Cook for 2 minutes. Cool a little. Stir in 5 tablespoons of sugar and the egg yolks and pour into the pastry shell. In a separate bowl, whisk the egg whites until stiff. Gradually whisk in the remaining sugar and spread over the pie. Bake for 40 minutes. Remove from the oven and serve.

bakewell tart

easy

serves 4

20 minutes
+ 30 minutes
to rest

40 minutes

ingredients

PASTRY	FILLING
200 g/7 oz plain flour, plus extra for dusting	100 g/3½ oz butter
100 g/3½ oz butter, diced, plus extra for greasing	100 g/3½ oz brown sugar
50 g/1¾ oz icing sugar, sifted	2 eggs, beaten
finely grated rind of 1 lemon	1 tsp almond essence
1 egg yolk, beaten	75 g/2¾ oz ground rice
3 tbsp milk	3 tbsp ground almonds
4 tbsp strawberry jam	3 tbsp flaked almonds, toasted
	icing sugar, to dust

To make the pastry, sift the flour into a bowl. Rub in the butter. Mix in the icing sugar, lemon rind, egg yolk and milk. Knead briefly on a lightly floured work surface. Leave to rest for 30 minutes.

Preheat the oven to 190°C/375°F/Gas Mark 5. Grease a 20-cm/ 8-inch ovenproof flan tin with butter. Roll out the pastry to a thickness of 5 mm/¼ inch and use it to line the base and sides of the tin. Prick all over the base with a fork, then spread with jam.

To make the filling, cream together the butter and sugar until fluffy. Gradually beat in the eggs, followed by the almond essence, ground rice and ground almonds. Spread the mixture evenly over the jam-covered pastry, then scatter over the flaked almonds. Bake in the preheated oven for 40 minutes, until golden. Remove from the oven, dust with icing sugar and serve.

chocolate orange tart

	i n g r e d i e n t s	
easy		
	PASTRY	FILLING & ORANGE CREAM
	200 g/7 oz plain flour, plus extra	200 g/7 oz plain chocolate, broken into
serves 4	for dusting	small pieces
	100 g/3½ oz butter, diced, plus	2 eggs, separated
	extra for greasing	100 ml/3½ fl oz milk
30 minutes	50 g/1¾ oz icing sugar, sifted	100 g/3½ oz caster sugar
+ 30 minutes	finely grated rind of 1 orange	8 amaretti biscuits, crushed
to rest	1 egg yolk, beaten	1 tbsp orange liqueur
	3 tbsp milk	1 tbsp finely grated orange rind
1 hour		125 ml/4 fl oz double cream
		orange zest, to decorate

To make the pastry, sift the flour into a bowl. Rub in the butter. Mix in the icing sugar, orange rind, egg yolk and milk. Knead briefly on a lightly floured work surface, then leave to rest for 30 minutes. Preheat the oven to 180°C/350°F/Gas Mark 4. Grease a 23-cm/9-inch flan tin with butter. Roll out two-thirds of the pastry to a thickness of 5 mm/¼ inch, and use it to line the tin.

To make the filling, melt the chocolate in a heatproof bowl over a pan of simmering water. Beat in the egg yolks, then the milk. Remove from the heat. In a separate bowl, whisk the egg whites until stiff, then stir in the sugar. Fold the egg whites into the chocolate, then stir in the biscuits. Spoon into the pastry shell. Roll out the remaining pastry, cut into strips and form a lattice over the tart. Bake for 1 hour. To make the orange cream, beat together the orange liqueur, orange rind and cream. Remove the tart from the oven, decorate with orange zest and serve with the orange cream.

lemon tart

easy	
serves 4	
20 minutes + 1 ¼ hours to rest/cool	
1 hour	

ingredients

PASTRY
200 g/7 oz plain flour, plus extra
  for dusting
3 tbsp ground almonds
100 g/3 ½ oz butter, diced, plus extra
  for greasing
50 g/1 ¾ oz icing sugar, sifted
finely grated rind of 1 lemon
1 egg yolk, beaten
3 tbsp milk

FILLING
4 eggs
250 g/9 oz caster sugar
juice and finely grated rind of 2 lemons
150 ml/5 fl oz double cream

mascarpone or crème fraîche, to serve

To make the pastry, sift the flour into a bowl. Mix in the almonds, then rub in the butter. Mix in the icing sugar, lemon rind, egg yolk and milk. Knead briefly on a lightly floured work surface, then leave to rest for 30 minutes.

Preheat the oven to 180°C/350°F/Gas Mark 4. Grease a 23-cm/ 9-inch flan tin with butter. Roll out the pastry to a thickness of 5 mm/¼ inch and use to line the base and sides of the tin. Prick all over with a fork, line with baking paper and fill with baking beans. Bake for 15 minutes. Remove from the oven. Lower the temperature to 150°C/300°F/Gas Mark 2.

To make the filling, crack the eggs into a bowl. Whisk in the sugar, then the lemon juice and rind and cream. Spoon into the pastry shell and bake for 45 minutes. Remove from the oven and leave to cool for 45 minutes. Serve with mascarpone or crème fraîche.

peach & strawberry tart

		ingredients	
easy		PASTRY	FILLING
		200 g/7 oz plain flour, plus extra	175 ml/6 fl oz double cream
		for dusting	4 tbsp icing sugar
serves 4		100 g/3½ oz butter, diced, plus extra	1 tbsp peach liqueur
		for greasing	4 tbsp strawberry jam
20 minutes +		50 g/1¾ oz icing sugar, sifted	2 peaches, stoned and sliced
1¼ hours to		finely grated rind of 1 orange	100 g/3½ oz strawberries, hulled
rest/cool		1 egg yolk, beaten	and sliced
		3 tbsp milk	icing sugar, to dust
15 minutes			whipped cream, to serve

To make the pastry, sift the flour into a bowl. Rub in the butter, then mix in the icing sugar, orange rind, egg yolk and milk. Knead briefly on a lightly floured work surface, then leave to rest for 30 minutes. Preheat the oven to 180°C/350°F/Gas Mark 4. Grease a 23-cm/9-inch flan tin with butter. Roll out the pastry to a thickness of 5 mm/¼ inch and use to line the base and sides of the tin. Prick all over the base with a fork, line with baking paper and fill with baking beans. Bake for 15 minutes. Remove from the oven and reserve.

To make the filling, put the cream into a bowl and beat in the icing sugar. Stir in the peach liqueur. Spread the bottom of the pastry shell with strawberry jam, then spoon in the cream filling. Arrange the sliced peaches and strawberries over the top, then cover with clingfilm and refrigerate for 45 minutes. Remove from the refrigerator, dust with icing sugar and serve with whipped cream.

spiced apple tart

	ingredients	
easy	**PASTRY**	**FILLING**
	200 g/7 oz plain flour, plus extra	3 medium cooking apples
	for dusting	2 tbsp lemon juice
serves 4	100 g/3½ oz butter, diced, plus	finely grated rind of 1 lemon
	extra for greasing	150 ml/5 fl oz clear honey
20 minutes +	50 g/1¾ oz icing sugar, sifted	175 g/6 oz fresh white or
30 minutes	finely grated rind of 1 lemon	wholemeal breadcrumbs
to rest	1 egg yolk, beaten	1 tsp ground mixed spice
	3 tbsp milk	pinch of freshly grated nutmeg
35 minutes		whipped cream, to serve

To make the pastry, sift the flour into a bowl. Rub in the butter. Mix in the icing sugar, lemon rind, egg yolk and milk. Knead briefly on a lightly floured work surface, then leave to rest for 30 minutes.

Preheat the oven to 200°C/400°F/Gas Mark 6. Grease a 20-cm/ 8-inch flan tin with butter. Roll out the pastry to a thickness of 5 mm/¼ inch and use to line the base and sides of the tin.

To make the filling, core 2 apples and grate them into a bowl. Add 1 tablespoon of lemon juice and all the lemon rind, along with the honey, breadcrumbs and mixed spice. Mix together well. Spoon evenly into the pastry shell. Core and slice the remaining apple, and use to decorate the top of the tart. Brush the apple slices with lemon juice, then sprinkle over the nutmeg. Bake in the preheated oven for 35 minutes, or until firm. Remove from the oven and serve with whipped cream.

hot desserts

This chapter presents a truly spectacular selection of hot desserts for you to try, from delicious Pear Crêpes with Chocolate Sauce to a mouthwatering Blueberry Clafoutis. For fruit-lovers everywhere, these desserts are a veritable feast: pears, blueberries, raspberries, blackberries, strawberries, nectarines, pineapples, plums, peaches, bananas and apricots all vie for your attention. And for those who love the combination of chocolate and cream, the Profiteroles simply cannot be missed.

pear crêpes
with chocolate sauce

easy	
serves 4	
15 minutes + 30 minutes to chill	
35 minutes	

ingredients

CRÊPES
125 g/4½ oz plain flour
pinch of salt
3 eggs
250 ml/9 fl oz milk

2 tbsp lemon oil or vegetable oil

FILLING
250 g/9 oz dessert pears
8 cloves
3 tbsp currants
pinch of ground mixed spice

SAUCE
125 g/4½ oz plain chocolate, broken
   into small pieces
2½ tbsp butter
6 tbsp water

To make the crêpes, sift the flour and salt into a bowl. Whisk in the eggs and milk to make a batter. Cover with clingfilm and chill for 30 minutes. Heat a little oil in a frying pan until hot. Add a large spoonful of the batter and cook over a high heat until golden, then turn over and cook briefly on the other side. Cook the other crêpes in the same way, stacking them on a plate. Preheat the oven to 160°C/325°F/Gas Mark 3.

To make the filling, bring a pan of water to the boil. Peel and slice the pears; add to the pan with the cloves and currants. Lower the heat and simmer for 5 minutes. Remove from the heat, drain, and discard the cloves. Leave to cool a little. Oil an ovenproof dish. Stir the mixed spice into the fruit; divide between the crêpes. Fold the crêpes into triangles. Arrange in the dish and bake for 15 minutes. To make the sauce, melt the chocolate and butter with the water in a small pan, stirring. Serve the crêpes with the sauce.

warm fruit nests

easy

serves 4

15–20 minutes

17–18 minutes

ingredients

2–3 tbsp lemon oil
8 sheets of frozen filo pastry, defrosted
250 g/9 oz blueberries
250 g/9 oz raspberries
250 g/9 oz blackberries

3 tbsp caster sugar
1 tsp ground mixed spice

sprigs of fresh mint, to decorate

double cream, to serve

Preheat the oven to 180°C/350°F/Gas Mark 4. Brush 4 small tartlet tins with oil. Cut the filo pastry into 16 squares measuring about 12 cm/4½ inches across. Brush each square with oil and use to line the tartlet tins. Place 4 sheets in each tin, staggering them so that the overhanging corners make a decorative star shape. Transfer to a baking sheet and bake in the preheated oven for 7–8 minutes until golden. Remove from the oven and reserve.

Meanwhile, warm the fruit in a saucepan with the caster sugar and mixed spice over a medium heat until simmering. Lower the heat and continue simmering, stirring, for 10 minutes. Remove from the heat and drain. Using a slotted spoon, divide the warm fruit between the pastry shells. Garnish with sprigs of fresh mint and serve warm with double cream.

fruit skewers

very easy	
serves 4	
15–20 minutes	
10–12 minutes	

ingredients

SKEWERS
6 tbsp brown sugar
pinch of ground mixed spice
8 whole strawberries, hulled
3 nectarines, stoned and cut into bite-sized chunks
400 g/14 oz canned pineapple chunks, drained
4 plums, stoned and cut into bite-sized chunks
6 tbsp butter, melted

CHOCOLATE ALMOND SAUCE
125 g/4$\frac{1}{2}$ oz plain chocolate, broken into small pieces
2$\frac{1}{2}$ tbsp butter
6 tbsp water
1 tbsp almond liqueur, such as Amaretto

chopped mixed nuts, to decorate

Combine the sugar and mixed spice and spread out on a large plate. Thread the whole strawberries onto metal skewers, alternating with the chunks of nectarine, pineapple and plum. When the skewers are full (leave a small space at either end), brush them with melted butter, then turn them in the sugar until lightly coated. Transfer to a barbecue or preheated grill pan and cook, turning occasionally, for 8–10 minutes.

To make the sauce, gently melt the chocolate and butter with the in a small saucepan, stirring constantly, until smooth. Stir in the almond liqueur. Remove the skewers from the heat. Divide between individual plates, decorate with chopped mixed nuts and serve hot with the chocolate almond sauce.

stuffed pears

very easy	
serves 4	
15 minutes	
1 ¼ hours	

ingredients

100 ml/3½ fl oz clear honey
125 ml/4 fl oz maple syrup
1 tbsp lemon juice
4 tbsp water
½ tsp ground cinnamon

4 large pears
4 tbsp mincemeat

whipped cream, to serve

Preheat the oven to 160°C/325°F/Gas Mark 3. Gently warm the honey, maple syrup, lemon juice, water and cinnamon, stir well then pour into a glass jug. Core and peel the pears. Using a sharp knife, cut a small slice off the bottom of each pear so that each one will stand up straight. Spoon some mincemeat into the centres, then stand them in an ovenproof dish. Pour the syrup mixture over the top, then transfer to the preheated oven. Bake, uncovered, for about 1¼ hours, basting with the syrup from time to time, until cooked through.

Remove from the oven and transfer to individual serving plates. Serve warm, with generous spoonfuls of whipped cream.

profiteroles

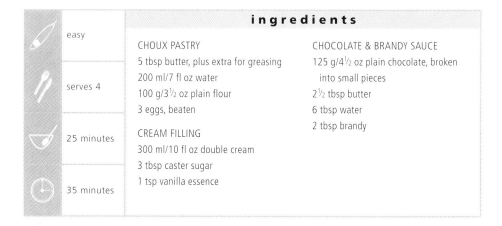

	ingredients	
easy	**CHOUX PASTRY**	**CHOCOLATE & BRANDY SAUCE**
	5 tbsp butter, plus extra for greasing	125 g/4½ oz plain chocolate, broken
serves 4	200 ml/7 fl oz water	into small pieces
	100 g/3½ oz plain flour	2½ tbsp butter
	3 eggs, beaten	6 tbsp water
25 minutes		2 tbsp brandy
	CREAM FILLING	
	300 ml/10 fl oz double cream	
	3 tbsp caster sugar	
35 minutes	1 tsp vanilla essence	

Preheat the oven to 200°C/400°F/Gas Mark 6. Grease a large baking sheet with butter. To make the pastry, put the water and butter into a saucepan and bring to the boil. Meanwhile, sift the flour into a bowl. Remove the pan from the heat and beat in the flour until smooth. Cool for 5 minutes. Beat in enough of the eggs to give the mixture a soft, dropping consistency. Transfer to a piping bag fitted with a 1-cm/½-inch plain nozzle. Pipe small balls onto the baking sheet. Bake for 25 minutes. Remove from the oven. Pierce each ball with a skewer to let steam escape.

To make the filling, whip together the cream, sugar and vanilla essence. Cut the pastry balls almost in half, then fill with cream.

To make the sauce, gently melt the chocolate and butter with the water together in a small saucepan, stirring, until smooth. Stir in the brandy. Pile the profiteroles into individual serving dishes or into a pyramid on a raised cake stand. Pour over the sauce and serve.

fruit pancakes

easy	
serves 4	
15–20 minutes + 30 minutes to chill	
15 minutes	

ingredients

PANCAKES
125 g/4½ oz plain flour
pinch of salt
2 eggs
300 ml/10 fl oz milk
2–3 tbsp vegetable oil

FILLING
1 banana
1 tbsp lemon juice

2 nectarines, stoned and cut into
    small pieces
1 mango, peeled, stoned and cut into
    small pieces
3 kiwi fruits, peeled and cut into
    small pieces
2 tbsp maple syrup

icing sugar, to dust

whipped cream, to serve

To make the pancakes, sift the flour and salt into a bowl. Whisk in the eggs and milk. Cover with clingfilm and chill for 30 minutes.

To make the filling, peel and slice the banana and put into a large bowl. Pour over the lemon juice and stir gently until coated. Add the nectarines, mango, kiwi fruits and maple syrup and stir together gently until mixed.

Heat a little oil in a frying pan until hot. Remove the pancake batter from the refrigerator and add a large spoonful to the pan. Cook over a high heat until golden, then turn over and cook briefly on the other side. Remove from the pan and keep warm. Cook the other pancakes in the same way, stacking them on a plate. Keep warm. Divide the fruit filling between the pancakes and fold into triangles or roll into horns. Dust with icing sugar and serve with whipped cream.

baked peaches with orange liqueur cream

	ingredients	
very easy	50 g/1¾ oz shelled pistachio nuts, finely chopped	HONEY SYRUP
		125 ml/4 fl oz water
	50 g/1¾ oz toasted hazelnuts, finely chopped	1 tbsp clear honey
serves 4		2 tsp freshly squeezed orange juice
	1 tbsp grated orange rind	150 g/5½ oz caster sugar
	1 tbsp brown sugar	pinch of ground mixed spice
20 minutes	pinch of ground mixed spice	
	4 large, ripe (but firm) peaches	ORANGE LIQUEUR CREAM
	1 tbsp unsalted butter	1 tbsp finely grated orange rind
30 minutes		125 ml/4 fl oz double cream
		1 tbsp orange liqueur

Preheat the oven to 180°C/350°F/Gas Mark 4. Put the nuts, orange rind, brown sugar and mixed spice into a mixing bowl and stir together well. Halve and stone the peaches. Remove a little of the flesh in the centre of each peach, chop into pieces, and stir into the nut mixture. Place a little of the mixture into the hollow in each peach. Transfer the peaches to an ovenproof dish and dot with butter. Bake in the preheated oven for 30 minutes.

About halfway through the cooking time, make the honey syrup. Put the water, honey, orange juice, caster sugar and mixed spice into a saucepan and bring to the boil, stirring constantly. Lower the heat and simmer, without stirring, for about 15 minutes.

To make the orange liqueur cream, put the orange rind and cream into a bowl and beat together, then stir in the liqueur. Remove the peaches from the oven and divide between serving dishes. Pour over the honey syrup and serve with the orange liqueur cream.

toffee bananas

easy	
serves 4	
20 minutes	
15–20 minutes	

ingredients

70 g/2½ oz self-raising flour
1 egg, beaten
5 tbsp iced water
4 large, ripe bananas
3 tbsp lemon juice
2 tbsp rice flour
vegetable oil, for deep-frying

CARAMEL
115 g/4 oz caster sugar
4 tbsp iced water, plus an extra bowl of
 iced water for setting
2 tbsp sesame seeds

Sift the flour into a bowl. Make a well in the centre, add the egg and 5 tablespoons of iced water and beat from the centre outwards, until combined into a smooth batter. Peel the bananas and cut into 5-cm/2-inch pieces. Gently shape them into balls with your hands. Brush with lemon juice to prevent discoloration, then roll them in rice flour until coated. Pour oil into a deep-fryer to a depth of 6 cm/2½ inches and preheat to 190°C/375°F. Coat the balls in the batter and deep-fry in batches for about 2 minutes, until golden. Lift them out and drain on kitchen paper.

To make the caramel, put the sugar into a small saucepan over a low heat. Add 4 tablespoons of iced water and heat, stirring, until the sugar dissolves. Simmer for 5 minutes, remove from the heat and stir in the sesame seeds. Toss the banana balls in the caramel, scoop them out and drop into the bowl of iced water to set. Lift them out and divide between individual serving bowls. Serve hot.

blueberry clafoutis

very easy	
serves 4	
15 minutes	
30 minutes	

ingredients

2 tbsp butter, plus extra for greasing
125 g/4½ oz caster sugar
3 eggs
60 g/2¼ oz plain flour, sifted
250 ml/9 fl oz single cream

½ tsp ground cinnamon
450 g/1 lb blueberries

icing sugar, to dust

single cream, to serve

Preheat the oven to 180°C/350°F/Gas Mark 4. Grease a 1-litre/
1¾-pint ovenproof dish with butter.

Put the remaining butter into a bowl with the sugar, and cream
together until fluffy. Add the eggs and beat together well. Mix
in the flour, then gradually stir in the cream followed by the
cinnamon. Continue to stir until smooth.

Arrange the blueberries in the bottom of the prepared dish, then
pour over the cream batter. Transfer to the preheated oven and
bake for about 30 minutes, or until puffed and golden. Remove
from the oven, dust with icing sugar and serve with single cream.

apricot crumble

	ingredients	
very easy	125 g/4½ oz butter, plus extra for greasing 175 g/6 oz brown sugar 500 g/1 lb 2 oz fresh apricots, stoned and sliced 1 tsp ground cinnamon	175 g/6 oz wholemeal flour 50 g/1¾ oz hazelnuts, toasted and finely chopped clotted cream, to serve
serves 4		
15 minutes		
30–35 minutes		

Preheat the oven to 200°C/400°F/Gas Mark 6. Grease a 1.2-litre/2-pint ovenproof dish with butter.

Put 3 tablespoons of the butter and 100 g/3½ oz of the sugar into a saucepan and melt together, stirring, over a low heat. Add the apricots and cinnamon, cover the pan and simmer for 5 minutes.

Meanwhile, put the flour into a bowl and rub in the remaining butter. Stir in the remaining sugar, then the hazelnuts. Remove the fruit from the heat and arrange in the bottom of the prepared dish. Sprinkle the crumble topping evenly over the fruit until it is covered all over. Transfer to the preheated oven and bake for about 25 minutes until golden. Remove from the oven and serve hot with clotted cream.

cold desserts

Cold desserts are delightful, and they can often be prepared in advance, leaving you more time for other things. If you are entertaining, this chapter presents an exciting selection of table centrepieces, from a rich Chocolate & Cherry Tiramisù to a spectacular Mixed Fruit Pavlova. The Cherry Baskets will look very impressive on your table, and so will the Blueberry Coeur à la Crème, while elegant Rose Petal Ice Cream will intrigue your guests. If you would prefer a lighter finish to your meal, try one of the refreshing sorbets in this section.

raspberry meringue

	ingredients	
easy	6 egg whites	DECORATION
	250 g/9 oz caster sugar	whole raspberries
serves 4	125 g/4½ oz ground almonds	fresh mint leaves
	1 tbsp butter, for greasing	
	850 ml/1½ pints double cream	
15 minutes + 2½ hours to cool/chill	5 tbsp icing sugar	
	600 g/1 lb 5 oz raspberries	
30 minutes		

Preheat the oven to 150°C/300°F/Gas Mark 2. Put the egg whites into a bowl and whisk until stiff peaks form. Gradually whisk in the caster sugar, then fold in the almonds.

Grease two 20-cm/8-inch sandwich tins with butter and line with greaseproof paper. Divide the meringue mixture between the tins and level the surfaces. Transfer to the preheated oven and bake for 30 minutes. Remove from the oven. Leave to cool on a wire rack.

Put the cream into a bowl, add the icing sugar and whip until softly peaking. Put one of the baked meringues onto a cake stand or serving plate and spread over a generous layer of the cream. Top with a generous layer of raspberries, then cover with the remaining meringue. Spread the remaining cream evenly over the top of the cake, and chill in the refrigerator for at least 2 hours.

Remove from the refrigerator, decorate with raspberries and fresh mint leaves and serve.

chocolate & cherry tiramisù

	ingredients	
very easy	200 ml/7 fl oz strong black coffee, cooled to room temperature	3 tbsp icing sugar
	6 tbsp cherry brandy	275 g/9 ½ oz sweet cherries, halved and stoned
serves 4	16 trifle sponges	60 g/2 ¼ oz chocolate, curls or grated
	250 g/9 oz mascarpone	
	300 ml/10 fl oz double cream, lightly whipped	whole cherries, to decorate
20 minutes + 2 hours to chill		
—		

Pour the cooled coffee into a jug and stir in the cherry brandy. Put half of the trifle sponges into the bottom of a serving dish, then pour over half of the coffee mixture.

Put the mascarpone into a separate bowl along with the cream and sugar and mix together well. Spread half of the mascarpone mixture over the coffee-soaked trifle sponges, then top with half of the cherries. Arrange the remaining trifle sponges on top. Pour over the remaining coffee mixture and top with the remaining cherries. Finish with a layer of mascarpone mixture. Scatter over the grated chocolate, cover with clingfilm, and chill in the refrigerator for at least 2 hours.

Remove from the refrigerator, decorate with cherries and serve.

pineapple cheesecake

	ingredients	
extremely easy	115 g/4 oz digestive biscuits, finely crushed	350 g/12 oz curd cheese
	4 tbsp butter, melted, plus extra for greasing	150 ml/5 fl oz double cream, whipped
serves 4		400 g/14 oz canned pineapple slices, drained and halved
	100 g/3½ oz caster sugar	
	juice of 1 lemon	pinch of freshly grated nutmeg, to decorate (optional)
20 minutes + 4 hours to chill	2 tbsp grated lemon rind	
	350 g/12 oz cream cheese	
—		

Put the crushed biscuits into a large bowl and mix in the melted butter. Grease a 20-cm/8-inch loose-bottomed cake tin with butter, then press the biscuit mixture evenly over the base.

Put the sugar into a separate bowl and stir in the lemon juice and the lemon rind. Add the cheeses and beat until thoroughly combined. Fold in the cream. Spread the cream mixture evenly over the biscuit layer. Cover with clingfilm and place in the refrigerator to chill for at least 4 hours.

Remove the cheesecake from the refrigerator, turn out onto a serving platter and spread the pineapple slices over the top. Sprinkle over a little grated nutmeg, if using. Serve immediately.

mixed fruit pavlova

easy	**ingredients**	
	6 egg whites	250 g/9 oz strawberries, hulled
	pinch of cream of tartar	and sliced
serves 4	pinch of salt	3 ripe peaches, sliced
	275 g/9½ oz caster sugar	1 ripe mango, peeled and sliced
	600 ml/1 pint double cream	2 tbsp orange liqueur, such
30 minutes	1 tsp vanilla essence	as Cointreau
+ 30 minutes to cool	2 kiwi fruits, peeled and sliced	fresh mint leaves, to decorate
3 hours		

Preheat the oven to 110°C/225°F/Gas Mark ¼. Line 3 baking sheets with baking paper, then draw a 22-cm/8½-inch circle in the centre of each one. Beat the egg whites into stiff peaks. Mix in the cream of tartar and salt. Gradually add 200 g/7 oz of sugar. Beat for 2 minutes until glossy. Fill a piping bag with the meringue mixture and pipe enough to fill each circle, doming them slightly in the centre. Bake for 3 hours. Remove from the oven. Leave to cool.

Whip together the cream and vanilla essence with 75 g/2½ oz of sugar. Put the fruit into a separate bowl and stir in the liqueur. Put one meringue circle onto a serving plate, then spread over one-third of the sugared cream. Spread over one-third of the fruit, then top with a meringue circle. Spread over another third of cream, then another third of fruit. Top with the last meringue circle. Spread over the remaining cream, followed by the remaining fruit. Decorate with mint leaves and serve.

sherry trifle

easy	
serves 4	
15 minutes + 4½ hours to cool/chill	
5 minutes	

ingredients

FRUIT LAYER
6 trifle sponge cakes
2 tbsp strawberry jam
6 large strawberries, hulled and sliced
2 bananas, peeled and sliced
400 g/14 oz canned sliced
    peaches, drained
6 tbsp sherry

CUSTARD LAYER
250 ml/9 fl oz double cream
1 tsp vanilla essence
3 egg yolks
4 tbsp caster sugar

TOPPING
300 ml/10 fl oz double cream
2 tbsp caster sugar

toasted, chopped mixed nuts,
    to decorate

To make the fruit layer, spread the sponge cakes with jam, cut into bite-sized pieces and arrange in the bottom of a glass serving bowl. Scatter over the fruit, pour over the sherry and reserve.

To make the custard, put the cream and vanilla essence into a saucepan and bring almost to the boil over a low heat. Meanwhile, put the egg yolks and sugar into a basin and whisk together well. Remove the cream from the heat and gradually stir into the egg mixture. Return the mixture to the pan and warm over a low heat, stirring, until thickened. Remove the custard from the heat and leave to cool for 30 minutes, then pour it evenly over the fruit layer. Cover with clingfilm and chill for 2½ hours.

Remove the trifle from the refrigerator. To make the topping, whip together the cream and sugar, then spread it evenly over the custard layer. Scatter over the toasted, chopped mixed nuts, then cover again with clingfilm and chill for a further 1½ hours. Serve chilled.

cherry baskets

		ingredients	
easy		BASKETS	FILLING
		3 tbsp unsalted butter, plus extra	300 g/10½ oz cherries, stoned
serves 4		for greasing	1 tbsp cherry brandy
		3 tbsp caster sugar	150 ml/5 fl oz double cream, whipped
		4 tbsp golden syrup	
25 minutes		½ tsp ground mixed spice	GLAZE
+ 1 hour		1 tsp almond essence	150 g/5½ oz redcurrant jelly
to set		1 tbsp cherry brandy	1 tbsp water
		5 tbsp plain flour, sifted	
20 minutes			

To make the baskets, put the butter, sugar and syrup in a saucepan and stir over a medium heat until melted. Simmer for 3 minutes, then remove from the heat. Stir in the spice, almond essence and brandy. Gradually mix in the flour and leave for 10 minutes.

Preheat the oven to 180°C/350°F/Gas Mark 4. Grease a large baking sheet with butter. Drop enough of the mixture onto the sheet to make 4 circles, 10 cm/4 inches in diameter, leaving space for each of them to expand. Shape the remaining mixture into 4 'handles' and lay them separately on the baking sheet. Bake for 15 minutes or until golden. Remove from the oven, then mould the basket shapes over the bottoms of 4 cups. Remove the baskets, add the handles and press to secure. Leave for 1 hour to set.

To make the filling, mix the cherries with the brandy. Spoon cream into each basket and top with the cherries. To glaze, melt the redcurrant jelly with the water and brush over the cherries. Serve.

raspberry brûlées

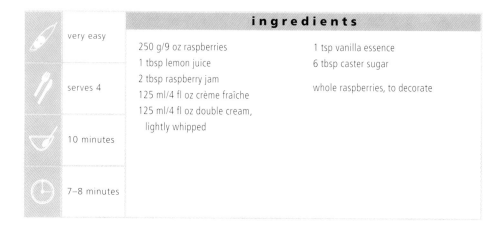

very easy	
serves 4	
10 minutes	
7–8 minutes	

ingredients

250 g/9 oz raspberries
1 tbsp lemon juice
2 tbsp raspberry jam
125 ml/4 fl oz crème fraîche
125 ml/4 fl oz double cream,
  lightly whipped

1 tsp vanilla essence
6 tbsp caster sugar

whole raspberries, to decorate

Put the raspberries and lemon juice into a saucepan and stir over a low heat for about 5 minutes until they start to soften. Remove from the heat, stir in the jam, then divide between 4 ramekins.

Preheat the grill to hot. In a bowl, mix together the crème fraîche, cream and vanilla essence. Spoon the mixture over the raspberries and level the surfaces. Sprinkle the caster sugar over the top, allowing 1 ½ tablespoons per ramekin. Cook under the preheated grill, as close to the flames or element as possible, for 2–3 minutes, until the sugar caramelizes. Remove from the grill, decorate with whole raspberries and serve immediately. Alternatively, to serve chilled, leave to cool to room temperature, then cover with clingfilm and place in the refrigerator to chill for 3–4 hours.

rich chocolate mousses

		ingredients	
easy		300 g/10½ oz plain chocolate (at least 70% cocoa solids)	1 tbsp brandy
serves 4		1½ tbsp unsalted butter	4 eggs, separated
10 minutes + 4 hours to chill			cocoa powder, to dust
5 minutes			

Break the chocolate into small pieces and put it into a heatproof bowl over a pan of simmering water. Add the butter and melt with the chocolate, stirring, until smooth. Remove from the heat, stir in the brandy and allow to cool a little. Add the egg yolks and beat until smooth.

In a separate bowl, whisk the egg whites until stiff peaks have formed, then fold them into the chocolate mixture. Divide 4 stainless steel cooking rings between 4 small serving plates, then spoon the mixture into each ring and level the surfaces. Transfer to the refrigerator and chill for at least 4 hours until set.

Remove the mousses from the refrigerator and discard the cooking rings. Dust with cocoa powder and serve.

blueberry coeur à la crème

		ingredients	
very easy	200 g/7 oz cream cheese		BLUEBERRY COULIS
	200 g/7 oz crème fraîche		200 g/7 oz blueberries
serves 4	2 egg whites, whisked		juice of ½ lemon
	2 tbsp caster sugar		1 tbsp icing sugar
	1 tsp vanilla essence		
20 minutes + 2 hours to chill			whole blueberries, to decorate
—			

Put the cream cheese, crème fraîche and whisked egg whites into a bowl; mix well. Stir in the sugar and vanilla essence. Line a large coeur à la crème mould with muslin, spoon in the cheese mixture and level the surface. Fold the edges of the muslin over the top.

Place a wire rack over a tray, then place the mould on the wire rack. Transfer to the refrigerator. Leave to drain and chill for at least 2 hours.

To make the coulis, purée the blueberries in a food processor, then strain through a sieve into a bowl. Stir in the lemon juice and icing sugar, then cover with clingfilm and chill until required.

To serve, carefully turn out the cheese from the mould and discard the muslin. Decorate with whole blueberries and serve with the blueberry coulis.

banana splits

		ingredients	
easy		4 bananas	CHOCOLATE RUM SAUCE
			125 g/4 $\frac{1}{2}$ oz plain chocolate, broken
		VANILLA ICE CREAM	into small pieces
serves 4		300 ml/10 fl oz milk	2 $\frac{1}{2}$ tbsp butter
		1 tsp vanilla essence	6 tbsp water
		3 egg yolks	1 tbsp rum
1 $\frac{3}{4}$–4 hours		100 g/3 $\frac{1}{2}$ oz caster sugar	
		300 ml/10 fl oz double cream, whipped	6 tbsp chopped mixed nuts,
			to decorate
5–10 minutes			

To make the ice cream, heat the milk and vanilla essence in a saucepan until almost boiling. In a bowl, beat together the egg yolks and sugar. Remove the milk from the heat and stir a little into the egg mixture. Transfer the mixture to the pan. Stir over a low heat until thick. Do not boil. Remove from the heat. Cool for 30 minutes, fold in the cream, cover with clingfilm and chill for 1 hour. Transfer into an ice cream maker and process for 15 minutes. Alternatively, transfer into a freezerproof container and freeze for 1 hour, then place in a bowl and beat to break up the ice crystals. Put back in the container and freeze for 30 minutes. Repeat twice more, freezing for 30 minutes and whisking each time.

To make the sauce, melt the chocolate and butter with the water together in a saucepan, stirring. Remove from the heat and stir in the rum. Peel the bananas, slice lengthways and arrange on 4 serving dishes. Top with ice cream and nuts and serve with the sauce.

rose petal ice cream

easy	
serves 4	
1¾–4 hours	
5 minutes	

ingredients

300 ml/10 fl oz milk
2 tbsp coconut cream
3 egg yolks
100 g/3½ oz caster sugar
300 ml/10 fl oz double cream, whipped
1 tbsp rose water

DECORATION
grated fresh coconut
rose petals

Pour the milk into a saucepan, stir in the coconut cream and heat gently until almost boiling. In a bowl, beat together the egg yolks and sugar. Remove the milk from the heat and stir a little into the egg mixture. Transfer the mixture to the pan and stir over a low heat until thickened and smooth. Do not let it boil. Remove from the heat and leave to cool for 30 minutes. Fold in the cream, then stir in the rose water. Cover with clingfilm and chill for 1 hour.

Remove from the refrigerator. Transfer into an ice cream maker and process for 15 minutes. Alternatively, transfer into a freezerproof container and freeze for 1 hour, then place in a bowl and beat to break up the ice crystals. Put back in the container and freeze for 30 minutes. Repeat twice more, freezing for 30 minutes and whisking each time. Store in the freezer until required.

Remove from the freezer and scoop into serving dishes. Scatter over the grated coconut and rose petals and serve immediately.

peach & banana sorbet

very easy	
serves 4	
20 minutes + 4 hours to freeze	
—	

ingredients

4 large peaches
2 bananas
1 tbsp peach brandy

fresh mint leaves, to decorate

Peel and stone the peaches, then cut the flesh into small chunks. Arrange them in a single layer on a tray. Peel and slice the bananas and arrange in a single layer on another tray. Transfer the trays to the freezer and freeze for 4 hours.

Remove the frozen peaches and bananas from the freezer and transfer to a food processor. Pour in the peach brandy and process until the mixture is smooth. Store in the freezer until required.

Scoop the sorbet into serving bowls, decorate with fresh mint leaves and serve immediately.

orange sorbet

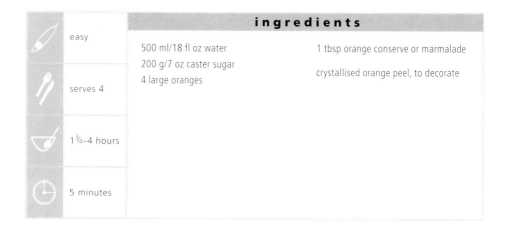

		ingredients	
easy		500 ml/18 fl oz water	1 tbsp orange conserve or marmalade
serves 4		200 g/7 oz caster sugar	crystallised orange peel, to decorate
		4 large oranges	
1¾–4 hours			
5 minutes			

Heat the water and sugar in a saucepan over a low heat, stirring, until the sugar has dissolved. Bring to the boil, then continue to boil without stirring for 2 minutes. Remove from the heat and pour the mixture into a heatproof, non-metallic (glass or ceramic) bowl, which will not react with acid. Leave to cool to room temperature.

Grate the rind from 2 of the oranges, then extract the juice from all 4. Mix the juice, rind and orange conserve in a bowl, then stir into the sugar syrup. Cover with clingfilm and chill for 1 hour. Transfer into an ice cream maker and process for 15 minutes. Alternatively, transfer into a freezerproof container and freeze for 1 hour, then place in a bowl and beat to break up the ice crystals. Put back in the container and freeze for 30 minutes. Repeat twice more, freezing for 30 minutes and whisking each time. Store in the freezer until required.

Remove from the freezer and scoop into serving bowls. Decorate with crystallised orange peel and serve.

index